MW00791051

# The Narrow Gate

# The Narrow Gate

Matthew J. Fratus

RESOURCE *Publications* • Eugene, Oregon

THE NARROW GATE

Copyright © 2023 Matthew J. Fratus. All rights reserved. Except for brief quotations in critical publications or reviews, no part of this book may be reproduced in any manner without prior written permission from the publisher. Write: Permissions, Wipf and Stock Publishers, 199 W. 8th Ave., Suite 3, Eugene, OR 97401.

Resource Publications
An Imprint of Wipf and Stock Publishers
199 W. 8th Ave., Suite 3
Eugene, OR 97401

www.wipfandstock.com

PAPERBACK ISBN: 978-1-6667-8775-7
HARDCOVER ISBN: 978-1-6667-8776-4
EBOOK ISBN: 978-1-6667-8777-1

VERSION NUMBER 09/01/23

Dedicated to my parents in Christ
Don and Jeanette,
who adopted me from the darkness.

&

A very special THANK YOU to the world's deepest pre-reader,
India Jones.

# Contents

# Author's Note

It is a near indescribable joy to have an opportunity to take what the Holy Spirit gives us and put it to paper. I consider it an honor among honors, personally. This is now my third published book of poetry. Like the two before, this was a work achieved in the bowels of deep sickness. In 2019, I received a vision from the Lord that on my 40th year, He would call me closer to Him. I remember my 40th birthday like it was yesterday. I woke excited, not quite sure what to expect from the Lord. I had family in town for the event, which added to the excitement. But, as the day went about, I started to feel unwell. I was tired, sluggish and my brain just seemed to be overwhelmed with the smallest of tasks. That evening, we made plans to eat at my favorite restaurant. When the times came however, I couldn't eat a thing. Instead, I went home and crawled into bed. Later in the evening, I went to use the restroom and the last thing I recall, was my wife panicked, trying to lift me off the bathroom floor. Somehow, I had fainted and fallen backwards, striking my head on our toilet. Suffice to say, this was not how I was expecting to be called close to the Lord.

A few months later, after many different doctor appointments, it was discovered that I had been exposed to a hexavalent metal that had made its way into my bloodstream, brain, and central nervous system. The initial results were active pre-cancers in my colon, breast, head, soft tissue, eyes, and nose. These were just the beginning. As the neoplasms were removed one by one, and the metal was chelated from my body, I was left with a life-changing neurological diagnosis that would cost me my 20-year career and the abundant life I was pursuing at that time. As everything I had worked to gain, began slipping away from me, it was becoming clear that the Lord was calling these things to happen. I found myself in the ashes of my former life, reading and relying on God's word more than I ever had before. When the word of God is all you have, it should be seen in the light that it is. . . As a life preserver. As I clung to that preserver, floating in a sea of unsureness, I began to see that the life I was called away from, while certainly fruitful for me, bore no fruit for the Lord. There was nothing in my daily executive pursuits to make the company I was employed with profitable, that profited the kingdom of God. Every previous communication attempt from God to me, had fallen on deaf ears and a hardened heart. And as I've learned, if we choose to ignore God's voice, He will always turn up the volume in hopes of rescuing those He is pursuing. I don't believe the Lord wanted to call me close through sickness. I do believe that I had become so detached from Him, that this was the only way He *could* call me back. And call me back He did. After years in this battle, I was given my calling. I created Zeal Artistry; a digital artwork studio with nothing but God's word, over my photos and digital creations. I was given poetry to share with the world, as a testimony to God. At the time of my writing this, Zeal Artistry reaches over a thousand people a day through our combined ministerial efforts. All of this was born from a promise of calling me closer, and through a painful return to the Lord. I'm very blessed to have a thorn in my flesh, as Paul was given. We who believe, do our best work under duress. It is in our weakness, where our God is made strong. I hope you are as moved by this work of poetry as I was when I wrote it. May God bless you abundantly with truth and grace in all you do for Him. Praise be to Him. These are His words.

# Introduction

## "I Never knew You, Depart from Me."

Matthew 7:22. . . When I think of this scripture, it gives me pause. Imagine devoting your entire life to what you thought was ministry, only to find in the end, you never actually knew the savior you professed to live by . . . Many scriptures can elicit emotions, but few hold the weight on my soul, that Matthew 7:22 holds. It truly is a gut-check. Afterall, we're saved by grace. No man can earn what we have received freely. So how then, can someone verbalize their love for Jesus and not be afforded His grace? How can that be? This sobering scripture is again reflected in Matthew 25:31. And, just as it is with scripture, a little more reading and we find our answer to the question that burns. . .

Jesus says in Matthew 25:31–46, "When the Son of Man comes in his glory, and all the angels with him, he will sit on his glorious throne. All the nations will be gathered before him, and he will separate the people one from another as a shepherd separates *the sheep from the goats*. He will put the sheep on his right and the goats on his left. "Then the King will say to those on his right, 'Come, you who are blessed by my Father; take your inheritance, the kingdom prepared for you since the creation of the world. For I was hungry, and you gave me something to eat, I was thirsty, and you gave me something to drink, I was a stranger and you invited me in, I needed clothes, and you clothed me, I was sick and you looked after me, I was in prison and you came to visit me.' "Then the righteous will answer him, 'Lord, when did we see you hungry and feed you, or thirsty and give you something to drink? When did we see you a stranger and invite you in, or needing clothes and clothe you? When did we see you sick or in prison and go to visit you?' "The King will reply, 'Truly I tell you, whatever you did for one of the least of these brothers and sisters of mine, you did for me.' "Then he will say to those on his left, 'Depart from me, you who are cursed, into the eternal fire prepared for the devil and his angels. For I was hungry, and you gave me nothing to eat, I was thirsty, and you gave me nothing to drink, I was a stranger, and you did not invite me in, I needed clothes, and you did not clothe me, I was sick and in prison, and you did not look after me.' "They also will answer, 'Lord, when did we see you hungry or thirsty, or a stranger or needing clothes, or sick or in prison, and did not help you?' "He will reply, 'Truly I tell you, whatever you did not do for one of the least of these, you did not do for me.' "Then they will go away to eternal punishment, but the righteous to eternal life."

Therein lies to crux. Jesus did more for us than any person will ever do. His perfect sacrifice gives us eternal life. But this gift, that was so freely given, came with expectations. The first of which, is that if we're saved by grace and have freely received, we should freely give, preaching the gospel and making disciples of all nations. If we have received Christ in our hearts, we're expected to live as if He dwells inside of us, with love, compassion, and a willingness to serve everyone around us. Certainly, we should strive to produce fruit for a kingdom, whose return is imminent. That's why we're told in the Olivet Discourse to keep watch. To care for the servants around us and to be ready. This was the very first messages (the Epistles) from the Apostles to the first churches. But even way back then, the message of the Apostles was challenged by the voice of the goats.

Oh, the goats. I'm going to share my observations from ministry about the goats. This book largely paints a vivid and unapologetic picture of this group. Goats are steeped in the very religion Jesus came to deliver His sheep from. Being both prideful and stubborn, they have worldly tendencies that hinder their ability to live for Christ, beyond just their words. Under the banner of Christ, the goats always seem more devout in the pursuit of theology, than the pursuit of love, mercy, or God's wisdom. They tend to self-justify. They are quick to speak and slow to listen. They're prideful, feeling as though the Lord has given them the secret of His holy wisdom, or permission to do what His holy words say, otherwise. They don't gently correct, they bully and ridicule. They measure themselves against others and boast in their accomplishments. They hold others to impossible standards based on their interpretations of scripture, but they themselves do not apply what they teach. And when the prideful goat is not agreed with, they insult others by saying things like, "Read your Bible!", or "Get some wisdom". Away from what we see, a goat is a person that is so confident in themself, they don't see the need to seek God's wisdom before they insult someone made in God's image. They may never admit it, but deep down, I believe many from this group feel that they've somehow earned what Christ gave, through their imagined piety. Unfortunately, through their work, no souls are brought to Christ. They are fruitless trees, promising weary travelers' nourishment and deceiving even themselves with nothing of sustenance to offer. And if that wasn't bad enough, they do it all in the name of Christ, in the sight of others. They sully the name of Christ. Woe to the goats. Woe.

The sheep, however, know the Shepherd's voice. They live like they know the Shepherd is watching them, enduring the narrow path, while striving to enter through the narrow gate ahead. They know they are loved and because they've tasted that love, they are eager to give it, freely. They are gentle in nature. The sheep can certainly give an impassioned testimony, but their pride is largely surrendered. They seek repentance when they stray. They know they are saved by grace alone. They're merciful. The sheep embody the characteristics of the beatitudes. They have a joy that others take notice of—one that surpasses all reason and understanding. They have a light about them. The unmistakable light of Christ. Though they may wander and stray, they accept the Shepherd's forgiveness when He leaves the ninety-nine to find them.

When these two groups stand before Christ and He begins to separate them, I believe it will be a time of shock, for many. My time on social media has taught me that the world has no shortage of flashy, self-proclaimed "Prophets" and "Apostles". In 2 Corinthians

11:5, the Apostle Paul found himself up against their teaching, and referred to them sarcastically as "Super Apostles". But no matter what man chooses to call himself, he will stand before the Lord, only by what he is known as, to the Lord. And before the throne of Christ, whether grace or judgement, it is our Lord and Savior who will decide what flock we truly belong to. The heavy-handed opinion of the goats will hold no value on that day. And, the sheep that endured the narrow path and gate, will receive salvation in the presence of all.

Better
to be
called a
SHEEP
by the
world,

than a
GOAT
by the
Shepherd.

# Chapter 1

The Ever Faithful

# The Rose

(For Brittany, Matthew, and Cali)

Behind what some suppose may be.
Beyond the yellow rose they see.
Are those who know the older me.
A growing weed, in tone and deed.

I once produced a fruitless hate.
A deep despair that bore its weight.
An unbecoming mound of freight,
that breaks the hearts of those who wait.

The three, I see them wait for me,
to be the man I ought to be.
Less distraught and thoughtless.
Teaching what Christ taught to me.

Yet, as the seed inside
was deeply nurtured from His vine,
it became something anew
much too beautiful to hide.

And, I began to see,
what opposition tried to keep.
That from the very start,
His tender heart
was set on finding me.

And what was next?
This seed it dropped
and found a deep ravine,
where water met its every need
and made the shell release.

Out from where it dwelt
from the protection of its shell.
A bloom protrudes.
Beauty exudes.
New life begins to swell.

Its colored petals boast
that it's no longer just a seed.
A rose has grown beneath the road,
protruding through concrete.

And those who'd usually sweep
this little flower with their feet,
are the ones who are the first
to stop and smell its sweet release.

The three they see and praise,
for their wait was not in vain.
They knew the troubled seed
would bloom among the heavy rain.

Despite the heavy pain,
they endured that former weed.
Despite no fruit produced,
God chose to use that fruitless seed.

And if that holy gardener
can do this all for me. . .
Imagine what can happen
with your fraction of belief.

# By Grace Alone

My Sinful, chastened lifestyle
you shall follow me no more.
The whips to flesh they bare the mark
of all that was in store.

A punishment so fitting.
The wage of sin is death
and death wants to collect,
but I'm no longer in his debt.

I'm no longer left from wisdom.
Truth I now possess.
The words my spirit heard
is now the word that I confess.

The world will second guess
and that's a choice that all will make.
I choose to not refuse the truth,
I'm only saved by grace.

My savior took my place.
For that tree was meant for me.
The purple curtain tore
and now His spirit dwells in *we*.

He speaks His words when I am close
but when I stray, he seeks.
The shepherd leaves the ninety-nine
to find a single sheep.

And when I'm finally found,
there's no anger in his voice.
There's me around his neck
and a heavenly rejoice.

That is why our choice
may seem so foreign to a few.
Our savior simply does the things
no *man* could ever do.

# Delivered

I'm rescued.
I'm blessed.
I've accepted
His best.

And my worst
is the first
that my savior
forgets.

A confession
is expected,
nothing less
will I give.

But the best
of my story,
is in Christ
I now live.

The weight
of my savior,
is the feel
of His grace.

His burden
is gentle.
His light
is my haste.

He desires
my best,
both spirit
and flesh.

I rest
when I'm less
and He grants
my request.

The redeemed
that He uses,
preach out
from their pain.

We preach
from the path
that leads many
in vain.

That path
leads astray,
but the Lord
and His say,

is that *all*
are forgiven.
The price. . .
It was paid.

The imperfect
made perfect.
We can never
deserve it.

Yet still,
we are fervent
to offer
our service.

Yet below
the surface
is what you
Must see.

Yet, what
you encounter,
is not
for the weak.

Each member
of Heaven
is worthy
of death.

But it's grace
that now saves
by the name
we confess.

The sins
that would burn us,
now a
testimony,

of the lengths
that He goes to,
to return
those redeemed.

*Thank you, Jesus.*

# Ebb and flow

He pursued
Pursued me
He grew me
It fused me
To the truth
That he used
To turn
Ashes to beauty—

He chased
Chased after
Imagine
The whole pasture
With ninety-nine
Behind him
Yet It's this one
That He's after—

I sought
Only truth
His truth
His view
With the wisdom
He gives
When the faithful
Pursue—

I pursued
Pursued Him

I refuse
To refuse Him
Or reuse
The three nails
The world used
To rebuke Him—

I chased
Chased fast
Yet my pace
Placed me last
Until the grace
He gave
Had Paved
A narrow
Path—

I follow
The hallowed
From shallows
To shadows
Hollowed hearts
Cannot preach
Where we preach
From the gallows—

He returned
Returned to us
With a shout
He withdrew us
From the proud
And the loud
Who refused
And abused us—

# Hebrews 11

Some had remorse.
Others, regretted.
Many were stoned,
flogged and beheaded.
Some were impaled.
Some sawn in two.
Some were refused,
while some were removed.

Some called to trust.
Others called to wait.
All for a trait
that we now know as faith.
A longing to please.
A reverence of heart.
A convergence of narrow
from the wide, where we start.

Some told their stories.
Some told their fate.
All were a voice
for a path ordered straight.
Not all were murdered,
though many were killed.
But every life taken,
our maker fulfilled.

What they gave, instills.
An example to tell.

The endurance of saints
that draw from His well.
The story they told
is the story we tell.
We honor their words
and the faith that they held.

As our time begins,
It's their time to watch.
They cheer from the clouds
at the return of the lost.
They paid a cost,
but now stand at the gate.
Awaiting the saints,
the heroes of our faith.

Be
Not
Afraid

# Chapter 2

How they Wander

# Fear

You fear the room
where sound emits.
When empty,
"sound" should not exist.

You fear the home
that's boarded shut.
What could be there?
You don't know what.

You fear the "what"
you do not know.
You fear the unknown
and the known.

You know the fear
you feel inside
and fear the feelings
you can't hide.

All the while
you carry fear,
you feel it feeling
too severe.

Fear roots itself
to suffocate
the hope you have
that you are saved.

As it grows
and boldly stirs,
a sudden whisper's
gently heard.

When you hear it,
you rejoice!
That's your holy
savior's voice!

But yours are not
the only ears
that hear those blessed
words you hear.

Fear, he heard.
His roots, they die.
and so reveals
his many lies.

Fear runs and hides
from the light,
when our Christ
is in his sight.

When He shines bright,
fear knows you're saved.
Jesus makes
our fear, afraid.

# Darkness

Preach to me.
Preach to me.
Heaven,
bare your reach to me.
The darkness
has its teeth in me.
But there is no
retreat for me.

Preach to me.
Preach to me.
This needle,
has no peace for me.
It offers
lies that some believe.
But He has
made my body clean.

Preach to me.
Preach to me.
Her eyes,
they spy a married me.
She tempts
but my salvation speaks.
I rebuke
what lust could be.

Preach to me.
Preach to me.

The man
I love abuses me.
These bruises
and contusions, Lord.
Forgive me,
if I choose to leave.

Preach to me.
Preach to me.
Holy Spirit,
hear my need.
The wine tonight,
divine indeed.
Deliver this,
beyond my reach.

Preach to me.
Preach to me.
Oh, Lord Jesus,
I believe!
Call me on the water.
But should I sink
Lord,
reach for me.

# Woe

We each hear the words.
We each have a choice.
The lot has been called
by the sound of His voice.

The choice though is yours
as the choice will be mine.
Two voices call,
but one is divine.

The world, she's a vixen.
and she knows your name.
She'll call and she'll wail,
whether sunshine or rain.

And should you refrain,
she'll up her game.
Sending more sin
that you love, to your shame.

And just like the world
that's already lost,
you may choose not the word,
or the gift of the cross.

The Devil just watches.
Don't flatter yourself.
For many have willingly
chosen His hell.

And no matter how many
hymns they may know,
they'll never know Him
so they twist what He spoke.

But when those red words
are read and their heard,
the Word changes sinners.
Sinners can't change The Word.

# We Do

We pray for His will,
yet don't want to lift.
We don't want to work.
We taunt those who sift.

We pray for his peace
but refuse to shift,
away from the place
where the light is bereft.

We wail and we mourn.
We toss and we turn.
We hear what we hear
but we don't hear to learn.

The good that He gives us,
we feel that we've earned
and the life we've forgone
is still one that we yearn.

*Yet forgiven.*
*Forgiven.*
*Forgiven are we.*
*Saved from our fate*
*by the grace we receive.*

*Though to all it is free*
*and hard to conceive,*

*all He requires*
*is that we believe.*

We pray for our Lord
to take full control,
then hold to the thing
too afraid to let go.

We claim to have faith
greater than seeds,
but no mountain moves
when we point it to sea.

We talk about scripture.
Quick to recite,
but the words that you heard
aren't applied to our life.

*Yet forgiven.*
*Forgiven.*
*Forgiven are we.*
*Saved from our fate*
*By the grace we receive.*

*Though to all it is free*
*and hard to conceive,*
*all He requires*
*is that we believe.*

# Sincerely, the Shepherd

Dear little sheep,
dear little sheep.
Let them
not lead you astray.

By the love they possess,
for the world's treasure chest,
or the sweet little words
they say.

Dear little sheep,
dear little sheep.
The one before you
is greed.

But the Lord,
He provides,
and though they deride,
believe you have all that you'll need.

Dear Little sheep,
dear little sheep.
Be not of goats
or their flock.

For the shepherd
will separate all in the end,
and His sheep
must be of His stock.

Dear Little sheep,
dear little sheep.
A wolf should not there,
be embraced.

For the wolves they desire
the warmth of Hell's fire,
and none
will be given My grace.

Beloved little sheep,
beloved little sheep.
Keep your eyes
to the sky!

When all that you see,
reminds you of Me,
your redemption
it draws nigh.

# Prodigal

I'm leaving.
I've left.
Gone.
Heavy steps.
This world
is a chest
to explore.

The treasures?
Abundant!
You say,
*Love none of it.*
but when I do,
I only want more.

So, I set out
with no doubt.
My faith is devout!
I can have you
and *still* have the world.

I'm strong and I'm stout,
and though I am out
in this world,
swine
won't get
my pearls.

*Confidence is mine.*
*Fear's absent from mind.*
*His word is behind me,*
*I bind what I bind.*
*I am His servant.*
*His word is divine.*
*It goes where I go,*
*so I see when I'm blind.*

This world. . .
What a sight!
It offers delight.
Though some are not right
to partake in.

I know that I'm saved,
so, I try, and I taste.
For the Lord
will not
leave me
forsaken.

I take and receive
way more
then I need.
What stands
before me
is abundant.

I know I'm
forgiven,
for the way that
I'm living.
To give more thought to this
is redundant.

*Confidence is mine.*
*Doubt's absent from mind.*
*This world is before me.*
*No fault do I find.*
*I am His servant*
*but the world is divine.*
*It calls me to visit.*
*I should be just fine.*

I've enjoyed!
Overjoyed!
Indulged.
Yet, avoided
my conscience
and the voice from within.

And though
there is sin,
I can be
born again,
whenever I choose
to repent.

I know
I'm ok.
I still try to pray
and go to church
where they say,
"I'm forgiven".

But the further
I fall,
the less I recall
those words
from the Lord's
Great Commission.

*Confidence is gone.*
*Anxiousness abounds.*
*I'm now lost in this world.*
*I need to be found.*
*I was his servant*
*but He's not around.*
*I pray He returns me*
*to His holy ground.*

I've not found life
in a world so fallen.
There's no paradise
in a world so appalling.

All that there is in a world
gone wrong,
is an outstretched hand
with a hole in its palm.

And all that there was
in my many mistakes,
was the faith I was given
the moment I prayed.

I received just a nudge.
A seed in the rough.
But that seed that receded in me
was enough.

To redeem me from lust.
To redeem the once lost.
To humble the one
who once counted the cost.

And returned to the cross
the once *lost and done.*

He restores my soul.
His prodigal son.

# Chapter 3

Without Judgement

# The Sheep

Rejoice,
the master found me.
Rejoice!
I once was lost.
I'm placed around
the shepherd's neck
with no thought
of His cost.

Mine was
a rebellion.
I wanted
to explore.
I ventured further
from the herd,
each day
to gaze at more.

But oh, the world
that caught my eye
it proved
a fool of me.
Absent from
the shepherd
are mere sheep
protecting sheep

The grass I found
to graze in

tasted bitter
when I ate.
I see now why
the shepherd
always chose
the place to graze.

The water that
looked calm and cool
was anything
but this.
I couldn't see
what lurked beneath
when I
wanted a sip.

The nights alone
are cold and dark
without my
shepherd's fire.
I hadn't much
considered this,
among the
day's desires.

The predators,
they roar and scream,
eager for
their taste.
It's then,
my shepherd finds me,
and returns me
to His place.

But all I saw,
truly pales

to what I
witnessed next,
as my shepherd
brought me home,
wrapped tight
around his neck. . .

Many friends
were joyful.
Many of them
weren't.
Many thought
of me
as a sheep
not worth return.

They grumbled
when they saw
our shepherd
carry me with joy.
They didn't
find me worthy
of my shepherd's
sweet rejoice.

As I heard
their whispers echo,
sadness came
to me.
That's when
my shepherd
whispered words
that opened me, to see.

He told me,
"*keep no thought*

*but love*
*for others in your mind.*
*The sheep*
*that choose to judge you,*
*are the next*
*I'll need to find."*

# "We"

We judge the sins found in our view,
yet place no thought on what we do.

We point them out, expose their guilt!
Then hide the sinful church we built.

*"Your worship's such a blasphemy!"*
we say to them, while gnashing teeth.

If they don't believe how we believe,
their soul is doomed indeed by *"We"*!

*See my garment,*
*long and proud?*
*It screams importance*
*to the crowd.*
*When I call out*
*The crowd knows me.*
*I'm fruit*
*from the poisoned tree.*

Who are they to try and teach?
Who authorized these men to preach?

How dare they question what we say!
How dare they lead *our* flock away!

They can't behold God's holy truth.
They're not old, they're filled with youth.

These aren't the people God would choose!
They truly are confused.

*See my garment,*
*long and proud?*
*It screams importance*
*to the crowd.*
*When I rebuke you*
*all will see.*
*I'm fruit*
*from the poisoned tree.*

See me with my great rebuke,
for those who don't do what I do.

I know they way. Come follow *me*.
Infallible! Ask history.

What I decree, the Lord decrees.
I'm that important. Don't you see?

I'm what religion makes of "*We*",
fair to say, a Pharisee.

*See my garment,*
*long and proud?*
*It screams importance*
*to the crowd.*
*They see and know*
*we're quite religious!*
*Making God*
*in our own image.*

# Accepted

Man is not exceptional.
Except one.
Accept *that* one.
Accept the exception.
The exception accepts *you*.
All are accepted.
Not all are expected.
All are accepted,
except the excessive.
The excess of the successful.
The excessively lustful.
The expertly loveless.
The accepters of sin.
The love for acceptance.
Except, we can't accept it.
There's no exception.
He gives no extension.
What the Lord sets is accepted,
by the elect, who respect it.
About those elected. . .
Exceptional?
No
Acceptable?
Yes.
Accepted.

# Millstone

Stunned
by the silence.
This world
and its violence.
Who can be saved
with such sins behind us?

I hasten
my weep,
for a nation
that sleeps.
In dismay, from decay
by the secrets we keep.

But The Lord
says, "I see."
And He sees
to the deep.
To the darkest of lies,
that unfaithful men keep.

They retreat
from His peace
and release
hell beneath.
Giving no thought of the cost,
or the loss they bequeath.

And it's here

we see. . .
A generation
esteemed,
to carry the sins
of the ones they succeed.

Unreasoning
people,
developed
since youth,
to respond to the truth
as a form of abuse.

To reply
to authority
with anger
and rage.
The same as the one
whom their fathers gave praise.

They claim
as victims,
yet they
didn't bleed.
And wisdom is proven
to be lost in their deeds.

A deed
that breeds riot.
Their hate,
they don't hide it.
They excuse the abuse
they use, when defiant.

They cast
Accusations,

that the mass of us
hate them.
But truth only sounds abusive
to the two ears of Satan.

We know
whom we serve.
We know
what's at stake.
For its life and it's death
in the choice that we make.

But to those
who provoked,
for the sake
of a vote. . .
What a weight that awaits
when you're thrown from the boat!

# They

Those who suppose
we are here
to oppose,
should listen
and surrender
their rage.

Ours is a mission.
The Greatest
Commission,
to witness
to any
unsaved.

We did not
come to you
to reject and reprove.
To rebuke
or ridicule
your life.

We came
to explain
the choices you weigh,
should include
the truth
of Christ.

You should know
that He died,
not to deny us,
but to pry us
from death
in our sin.

And though
the saved
have shown you
their hate,
you'll *never* receive that
from Him.

No matter
what others
may make
you believe,
His is a truth
you can read.

You were a thought
in His mind,
when He bought
us each,
from the one
who deceives.

Forgiveness
is yours!
Hear
His implore!
He loves you!
Surrender your guilt.

And even if
every
Christian
condemns you,
Jesus,
He never will.

*We truly condemn ourselves*

# Exhortation

Dearest reader,

I implore you from the deepest part of my soul to ask yourself the simple question. . . "Am I saved?" Imagine you have two reserved seats. . . One is on a lifeboat and the other is on a sinking ship.

Are you hurting?

Are you tired?

Confused or discouraged?

You're in great company! At one point in their calling, so was every Biblical hero, Apostle, Disciple, Preacher, Pastor, and Priest our world has ever known.

That reserved seat on the lifeboat was paid for, by the blood of Jesus.

The goats may say, "You're not good enough."

But that simply isn't true.

None of us are *good enough.*

That's the secret.

We all need Jesus!

When you come to Him, He'll tell you what needs to be changed.

And together, a beautiful work begins.

The next page will help you begin that conversation.

A loving conversation, between a shepherd and His beloved sheep.

If you can't remember the date,

If you can't remember the time,

If you can't remember the moment,

Stop everything and say these words...


Jesus, I believe YOU are the Son of God,
that YOU died on the cross to rescue me
from sin and death and to restore me to the
Father. I choose now to turn from my sins,
my self-centeredness, and every part of my
life that does not please YOU. I choose
YOU. I give myself to YOU.


Don't ASSUME your salvation,

ASSURE it!

# SOME
## WILL HEAR MATTHEW 25:23
# SOME
## WILL HEAR MATTHEW 7:23
# SOME
## WILL STAND BEFORE GRACE
# SOME
## WILL STAND BEFORE JUDGEMENT
# SOME
## WILL BE SHEEP
# SOME
## WILL BE GOATS
# EVERY
## KNEE WILL BOW